I WOULDN'T LET... A PANDA LAUNCH A SPACECRAFT

By Paul Mason

Illustrated by Pipi Sposito

WAYLAND

First published in Great Britain in 2026
by Wayland
© Hodder and Stoughton, 2026
All rights reserved

Credits:
Series Editor: Melanie Palmer
Design: Lisa Peacock
Illustrations: Pipi Sposito

ISBN HB 978 1 5263 3090 1
ISBN PB 978 1 5263 3091 8

Printed and bound in Dubai

Wayland
An imprint of
Hachette Children's Group
Part of Hodder and Stoughton
Carmelite House
50 Victoria Embankment
London EC4Y 0DZ

An Hachette UK Company
www.hachette.co.uk
www.hachettechildrens.co.uk

The authorised representative in the EEA
is Hachette Ireland, 8 Castlecourt Centre,
Dublin 15, D15 XTP3, Ireland
(email: info@hbgi.ie).

MIX
Paper | Supporting
responsible forestry
FSC® C104740

CONTENTS

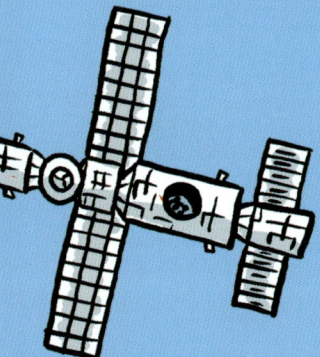
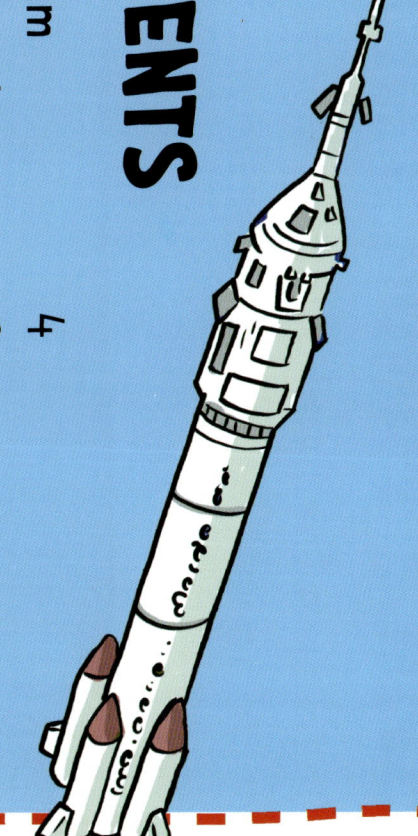

Space Panda's dream	4
Becoming an astronaut	6
Space Panda has liftoff	8
Escaping Earth	10
Space station ahoy!	12
Space station visits	14
Space Panda in the lab	16
Microgravity	18
A panda ... spacewalk?	20
Spacewalks	22
Dinner and wash-time	24
Living in space	26
Going home	28
Bonus panda facts	30
Glossary	31
Index	32

BECOMING AN ASTRONAUT

Becoming Space Panda isn't easy. Only the top candidates are selected to be an astronaut.

They have to be really fit ...

Huff ... puff ...

Beep! Beep!

Because astronauts do physical tests in space.

... and really smart! Astronauts run science experiments and mend complicated equipment.

JOBS IN SPACE

On a mission, there are two main jobs Space Panda could do:

1. PILOT
The pilot makes sure the spacecraft reaches its destination safely.

Here we go!

2. MISSION SPECIALIST
Mission specialists are often engineers, scientists or health experts. They maintain the spacecraft and perform experiments.

It DOESN'T need gravity to make webs.

SPIDER EXPERIMENT
DO NOT TOUCH

Obviously not.

SPACE FACT: OVER 600 PEOPLE HAVE TRAVELLED INTO SPACE SO FAR (BUT NO PANDAS - YET!)

SPACE PANDA HAS LIFTOFF

Space Panda – you're aboard the launch vehicle. Your space mission has begun!

The first part is easy. Pandas are excellent at lying down.

The spacecraft's rockets push against Earth's gravity.

"... 2 ... 1 ... Ignition."

Space Panda is pressed back against the seat.

"Being an astronaut is easy!"

The journey into space has begun.

"So far, this has been VERY simple."

Space Panda aboard

PANDA FACT: PANDAS SOMETIMES CLIMB TALL TREES, SO THEY DON'T MIND HEIGHTS.

ESCAPING EARTH

To reach space, you have to escape from Earth's gravity.

Gravity is a pulling force. All objects have gravity. Heavier objects have more gravity.

SPACE-SCIENCE TEST
Rank these objects in order of their gravity's strength*:

1 Yum! (panda)

2 Bamboo

3 Planet Earth

(*Answer on page 32)

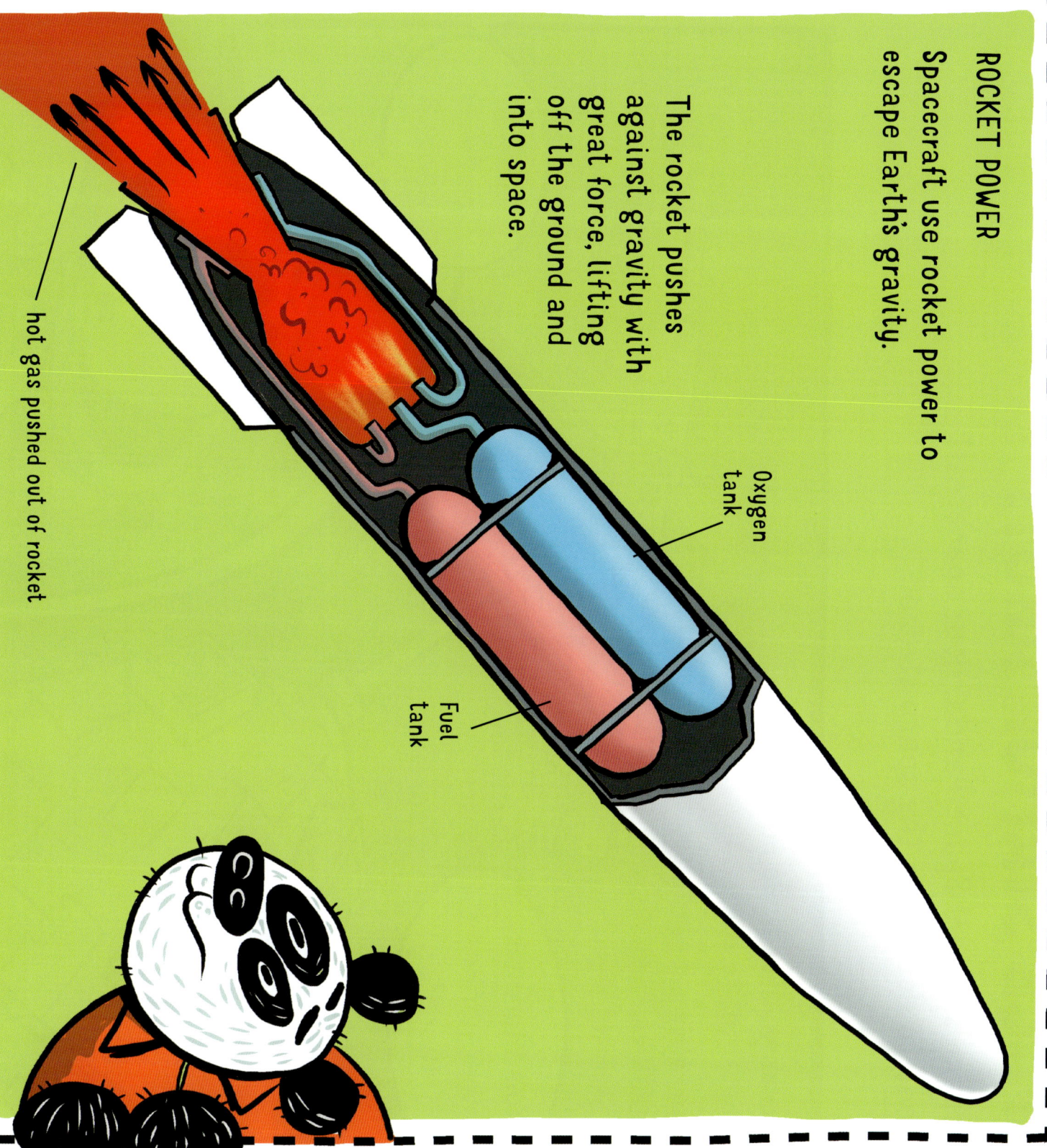

ROCKET POWER

Spacecraft use rocket power to escape Earth's gravity.

The rocket pushes against gravity with great force, lifting off the ground and into space.

Oxygen tank

Fuel tank

hot gas pushed out of rocket

As the rocket gets further from the surface, Earth's gravity gets weaker.

SPACE STATION AHOY!

A space station! Space Panda, your spacecraft needs to dock with the space station.

Docking takes three hours. It's important to stay awake for this.

"Will there be other pandas there?"

"No nap for THREE HOURS?"

PANDA FACT: MOST PANDAS ARE ASLEEP FOR AROUND 10 HOURS A DAY.

The spacecraft has to be steered into the docking port ...

It'll be fine.

... and controlling the little steering rockets is not easy.

OOPS!

ALERT! ALERT!

Fortunately, Mission Control can control docking from Earth.

Phew!

Space Panda has made it.

CLUNK!

PANDA FACT: PANDAS USE THEIR EXTENDED WRIST BONE FOR GRIPPING (THEY DON'T HAVE THUMBS)

SPACE STATION VISITS

Why would a spacecraft visit a space station? There are two main reasons.

1. CREW CHANGE
A space station's crew changes about every six months. Spacecraft bring new crew members. Then they take the old crew back to Earth.

2. RESUPPLY AND WASTE REMOVAL

Spacecraft bring fresh supplies. Waste (including squashed-down poo) is taken away.

On a space station, wee can be cleaned then re-used as drinking water.

PANDA FACT: PANDAS POO ABOUT 40 TIMES A DAY.

SPACE PANDA IN THE LAB

Now you're aboard the space station, Space Panda, it's time for some science experiments.

Next, let's do some reaction-speed tests.

"Green light!"

CLICK

Pandas don't really move that fast ...

For the last experiment, let's test how you sleep in space.

"Just try to get straight to sleep."

At last! A test I'll be good at.

MICROGRAVITY

Lots of space-station experiments are about the effects of not feeling gravity.*

Without ground to push against, you (and the space station) constantly fall toward Earth.

Don't worry! The space station is also moving AWAY from Earth at high speed.

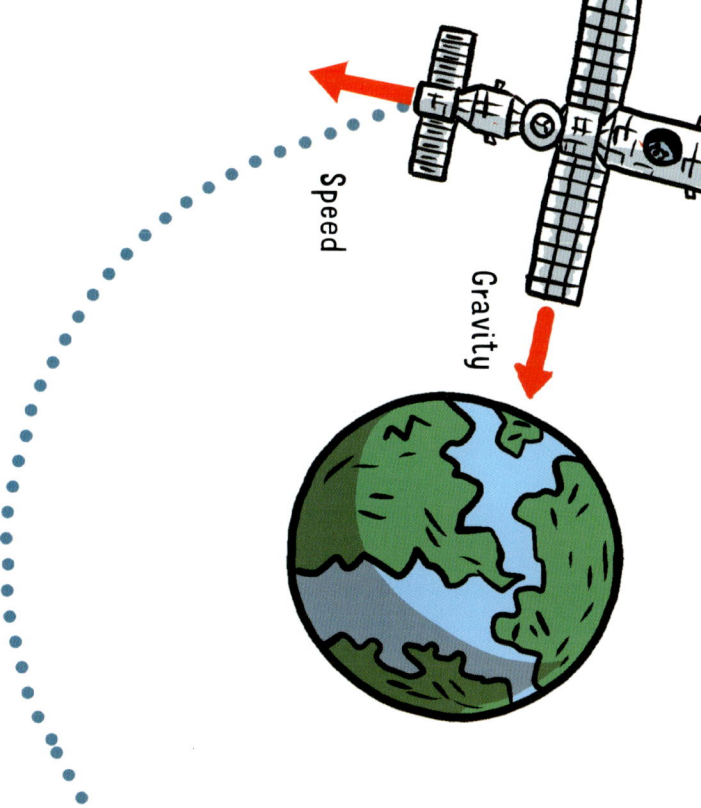

Space station's path

Speed

Gravity

The two forces balance – so aboard the space station, you can't feel either of them.

WHAT?

PANDA FACT: A PANDA'S TOP SPEED (ON EARTH) IS ABOUT 30 KPH.

A PANDA ... SPACEWALK?

Panda! It's time to leave the cozy space station and go for a spacewalk.

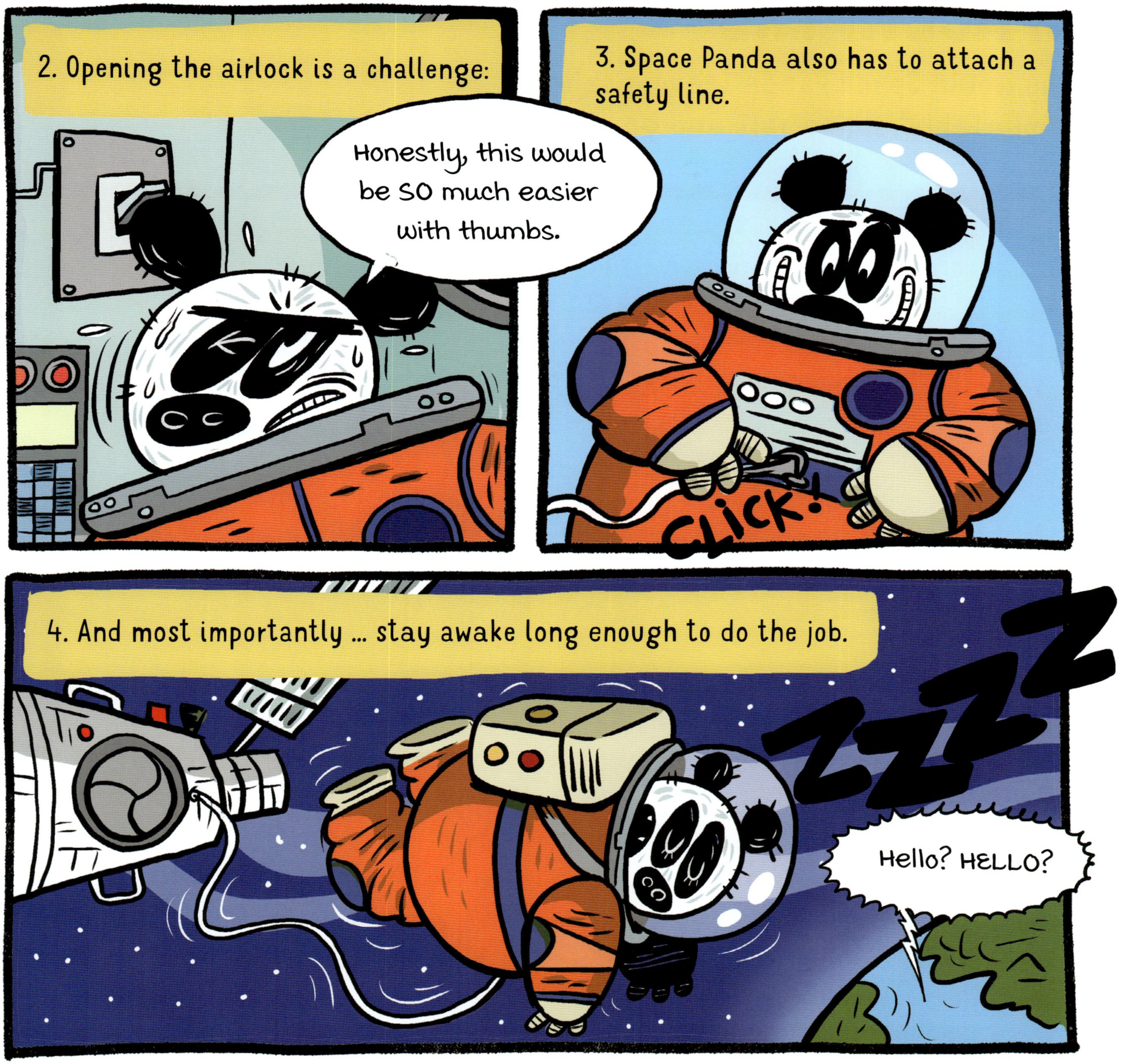

2. Opening the airlock is a challenge:

"Honestly, this would be SO much easier with thumbs."

3. Space Panda also has to attach a safety line.

click!

4. And most importantly... stay awake long enough to do the job.

ZZZZ

Hello? HELLO?

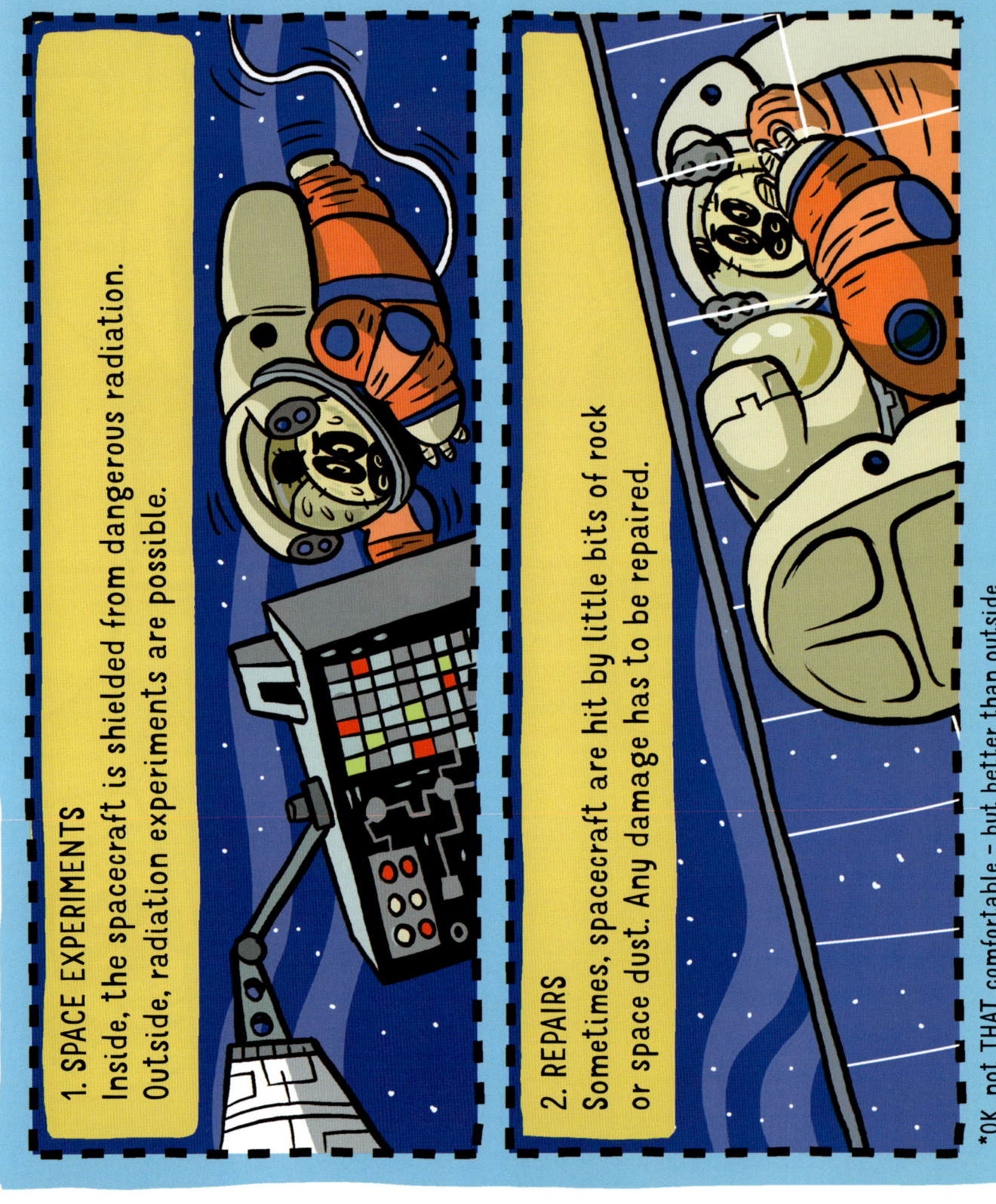

A SPACEWALK SUIT

Outside the spacecraft, your space suit keeps you alive:

- Backpack for oxygen, water and power
- Under-layer carries cooling water
- Gold-lined visor shields eyes from radiation
- Tough protective cloth
- Chest harness for safety lines/equipment

Whoo! Whee-hee!

FLYING FACT: AN EXTRA PACK CONTAINS SMALL ROCKETS – FOR FLYING THROUGH SPACE IN AN EMERGENCY.

DINNER AND WASH-TIME

Space Panda, your work is finished. It's time for dinner, and maybe a wash.

Eating in microgravity can be tricky. Food and liquid just floats off!

Oh, no! My dinner!

I'm REALLY hungry.

These bamboo shoots were MEANT for a science experiment, but...

Fortunately...

LIVING IN SPACE

Spending time in microgravity will affect Space Panda's body, as it does a human astronaut's body.*

Without gravity pulling blood downward, blood stays higher up in the body. This can cause:

Puffy faces

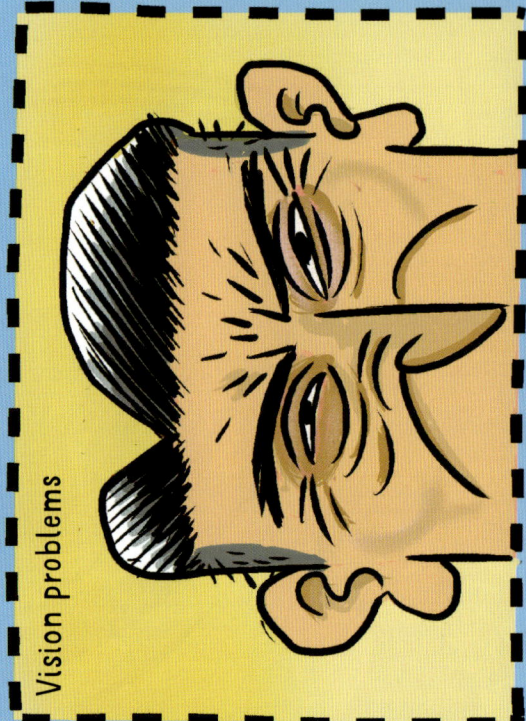

Vision problems

Skinny legs (or 'chicken legs')

BEFORE

Microgravity will affect Space Panda's body in similar ways.

*Pandas and humans are both mammals.

GOING HOME

Space Panda, it's time to climb back into your spacecraft and go home.

First, the spacecraft separates from the space station.

Ok!

The descent module speeds through the atmosphere.

Close to the surface, a parachute opens.

Shock-absorbing seats cushion Space Panda's landing.

Oof!

CRASH!

BONUS PANDA FACTS

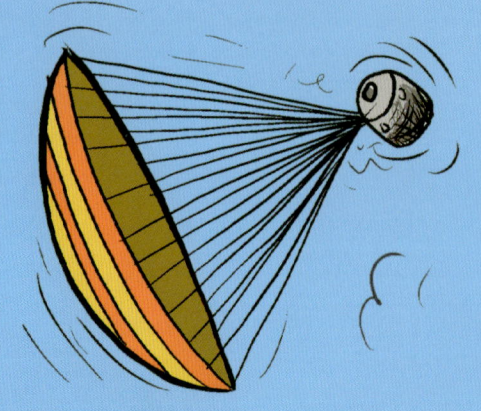

1. Pandas have eyes with vertical slits, like a cat's. It's because they are mostly active at night-time, and this helps them see better in the dark.

2. Pandas LOVE to roll around.

3. They are quite clumsy, and also seem to be fairly lazy.

4. Pandas spend 10-16 hours a day eating.

5. To stay healthy, pandas need to eat at least two different kinds of bamboo.

6. Pandas sometimes (though rarely) eat other shoots, leaves and roots, as well as pumpkin and kidney beans.

7. They mostly live alone, and mark their territory by rubbing their bottoms on rocks and tree trunks.

8. Pandas also sometimes wee doing a handstand against a tree, so that their marking is really high up.

9. The name for a group of pandas is an 'embarrassment'.

GLOSSARY

airlock – compartment or room with two doors. The doors are sealed so that air and other gases cannot pass through them

dock – attaches one object to another so that items or information can pass between them

engineer – someone who designs, makes or mends machines and structures

liftoff – the moment when a spacecraft leaves the surface of the Earth

maintain – keep working

microgravity – situation where only a tiny amount of Earth's gravity can be felt

mammal – animal that has some sort of body hair and feeds its young on milk from the mother

radiation – form of energy that spreads out from its source, such as sunlight. Some kinds of radiation are harmful to living things

rocket – long, thin flying object that is powered by burning fuel

space dust – small pieces of matter that drift through space

spacewalk – movement through space by a human who is outside a spacecraft

visor – see-through part of a helmet, which can usually be opened or closed

INDEX

airlock 21, 31
astronaut 4, 5, 6, 26
atmosphere 28

exercise 6, 16, 18, 27

forces 19

gravity 7, 9, 10, 11, 18, 19, 26

launch vehicle 8

microgravity 5, 24, 26-27, 31
module 28
muscles 27

oxygen 11, 23

parachute 28

radiation 22, 23
rocket 11, 13, 23

space dust 22
space food 5, 24
space station 12-13, 14-15, 19, 28
space suit 20, 23
spacewalk 20, 22

Answer to page 10: Least-powerful to most-powerful gravity: bamboo (2), panda (1), Earth (3)